EMINEM

Gareth Stevens
Publishing

By Roman O'Sorus

RIGHT ON!

Please visit our website, www.garethstevens.com. For a free color catalog of all our high-quality books, call toll free 1-800-542-2595 or fax 1-877-542-2596.

Library of Congress Cataloging-in-Publication Data

O'Sorus, Roman.
Eminem / Roman O'Sorus.
    p. cm. — (Hip-hop headliners)
Includes index.
ISBN 978-1-4339-6610-1 (pbk.)
ISBN 978-1-4339-6611-8 (6-pack)
ISBN 978-1-4339-6608-8 (library binding)
1. Eminem (Musician) 2. Rap musicians—United States—Biography. I. Title.
ML3930.E46O86 2012
782.421649092—dc23
[B]

2011022094

First Edition

Published in 2012 by
Gareth Stevens Publishing
111 East 14th Street, Suite 349
New York, NY 10003

Designer: Haley W. Harasymiw
Editor: Therese M. Shea

Photo credits: Cover background Shutterstock.com; cover, p. 1 (Eminem) Frederick M. Brown/Getty Images; pp. 5, 25 Vinnie Zuffante/Getty Images; p. 7 Barry King/Getty Images; pp. 9, 23 Kevin Winter/Getty Images; p. 11 Bill Pugliano/Getty Images; p. 13 Denis Doyle/AFP/Getty Images; pp. 15, 21 WireImage/Getty Images; pp. 17, 19 Frank Micelotta/Getty Images; p. 27 Christopher Polk/Getty Images; p. 29 Jeff Kravitz/FilmMagic/Getty Images.

Printed in the United States of America

CPSIA compliance information: Batch #CW12GS: For further information contact Gareth Stevens, New York, New York at 1-800-542-2595.

Contents

Three Names, One Star

Many stars change their names. The rapper Eminem is different. He uses many names. His real name is Marshall Bruce Mathers. He is also called Slim Shady.

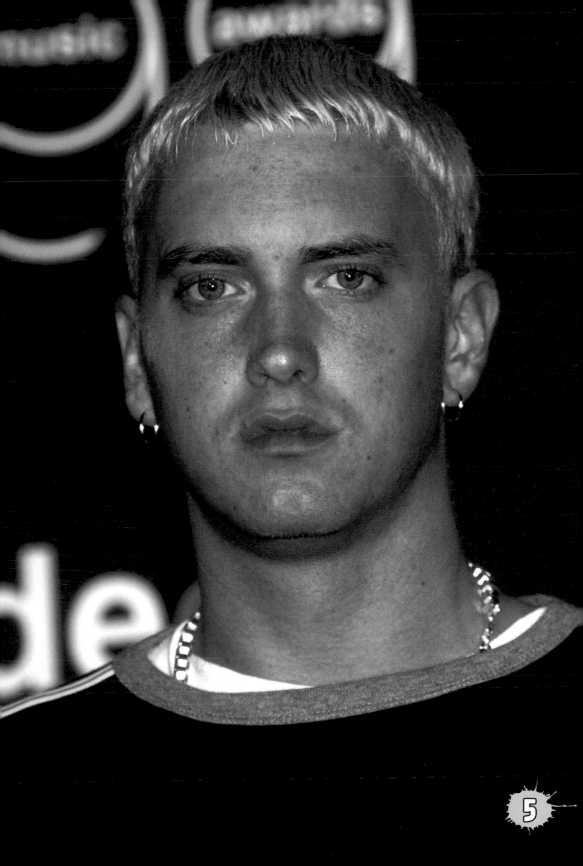

5

Marshall was born October 17, 1972. He lived in Kansas City, Missouri. He spent a lot of time in Michigan.

Rapping in Detroit

During his teens, Marshall lived in Detroit, Michigan. There, he began rapping with a high school friend. He called himself M&M. He later changed that to Eminem.

Eminem began to battle-rap with other artists. Battle-rapping lets judges choose the rapper with the best lyrics. Eminem was very good at battle-rapping.

11

Eminem was asked to join a rap group called the New Jacks. Then he joined another group called Soul Intent. Their first song came out in 1995.

Next, Eminem formed a group with a rapper named Proof. They were called D-12. Eminem had to work at another job after his daughter was born. He did not have much time for music.

15

Eminem was unhappy not making music. He rapped about his feelings. In 1996, he put out his first album. It was called *Infinite*.

Enter Slim Shady

Eminem began to rap more about his life. He used the name Slim Shady. In 1997, Eminem took second place at a rap olympics. He got a deal with a record company.

Rap superstar Dr. Dre worked with Eminem. He helped Eminem put out *The Slim Shady LP* in 1999. The song "My Name Is" was the biggest hit.

Dr. Dre

21

Rapping and Acting

Eminem's next record came out in 2000. It was called *The Marshall Mathers LP*. It was the fastest-selling rap album ever.

In 2001, Eminem starred in a movie based on his life. It was called *8 Mile*. He wrote a song for the movie called "Lose Yourself." He won Oscar and Grammy awards for it!

The rapper's next two albums were called *The Eminem Show* and *Encore*. Then, Eminem took a break from making music.

Still Topping the Charts

In 2010, Eminem's album *Recovery* topped the charts for 5 weeks. His biggest hit was "Love the Way You Lie" with Rihanna. What is next for this hip-hop superstar?

Rihanna

Timeline

1972   Marshall Mathers is born in Kansas City, Missouri.

1986   Mathers begins rapping as M&M.

1997   Eminem begins working with a record company.

1999   *The Slim Shady LP* comes out.

2000   *The Marshall Mathers LP* becomes the fastest-selling rap album ever.

2001   The movie *8 Mile* comes out.

2010   *Recovery* tops the charts for 5 weeks.

For More Information

Books

Abrams, Dennis. *Eminem*. New York, NY: Checkmark Books, 2008.

Hill, Z. B. *Eminem*. Philadelphia, PA: Mason Crest Publishers, 2012.

Websites

Eminem

www.billboard.com/artist/eminem/315925#/artist/eminem/315925

Read the complete list of Eminem's records, and find out how they did on the charts.

Eminem

www.mtv.com/music/artist/eminem/artist.jhtml

Read more about Eminem's life, and listen to his hit songs.

Publisher's note to educators and parents: Our editors have carefully reviewed these websites to ensure that they are suitable for students. Many websites change frequently, however, and we cannot guarantee that a site's future contents will continue to meet our high standards of quality and educational value. Be advised that students should be closely supervised whenever they access the Internet.

Glossary

award: an honor

LP: short for "long-playing record," which is another name for an album

lyrics: the words of a song

olympics: events in which people try to do better than others

record: a copy of music that can be played again and again

Index